Raging Hot Girls

Hot Sexy Lingerie & Swimsuit Girls Models Pictures

By **PHOTO ART LOVER**

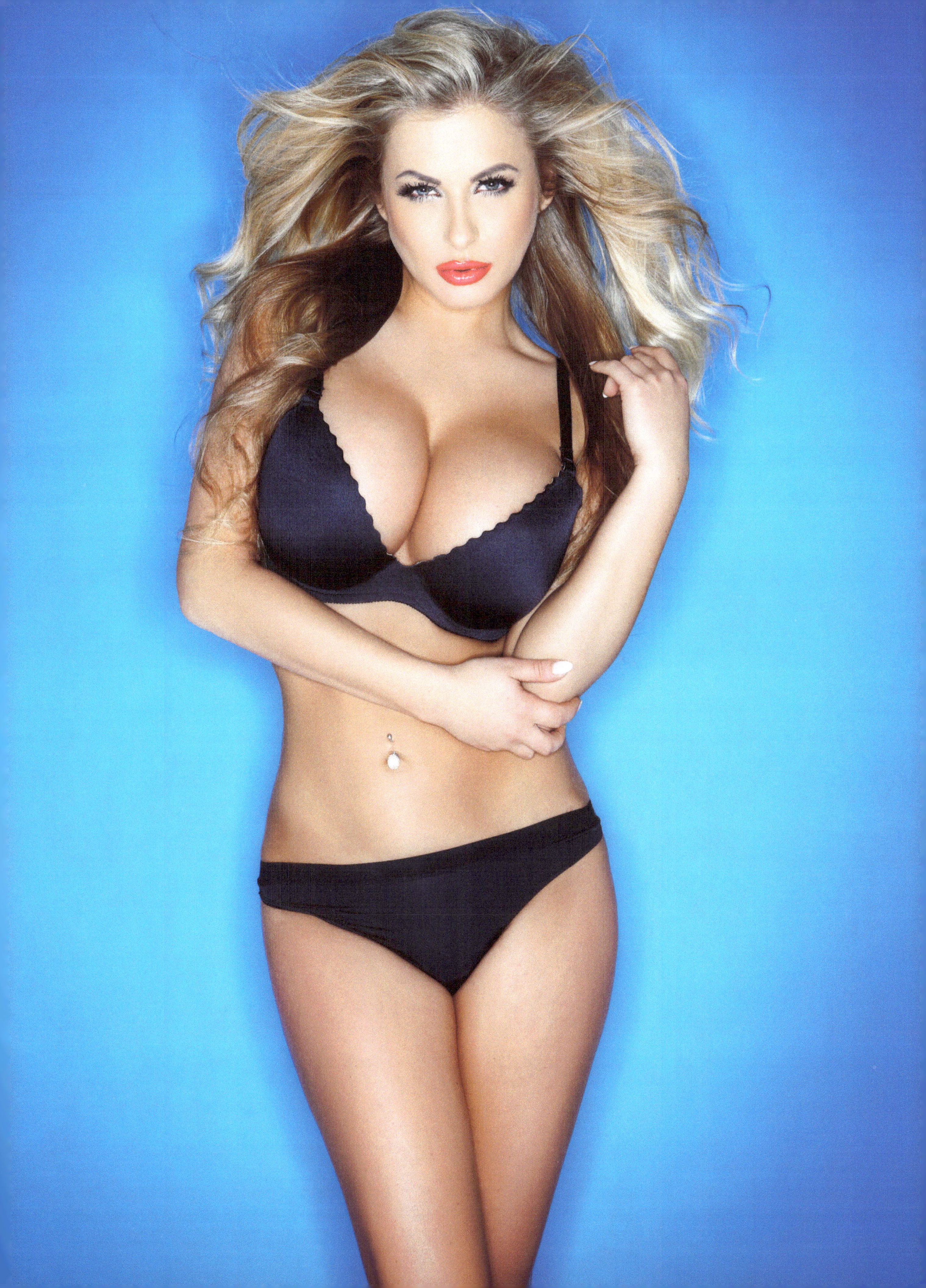

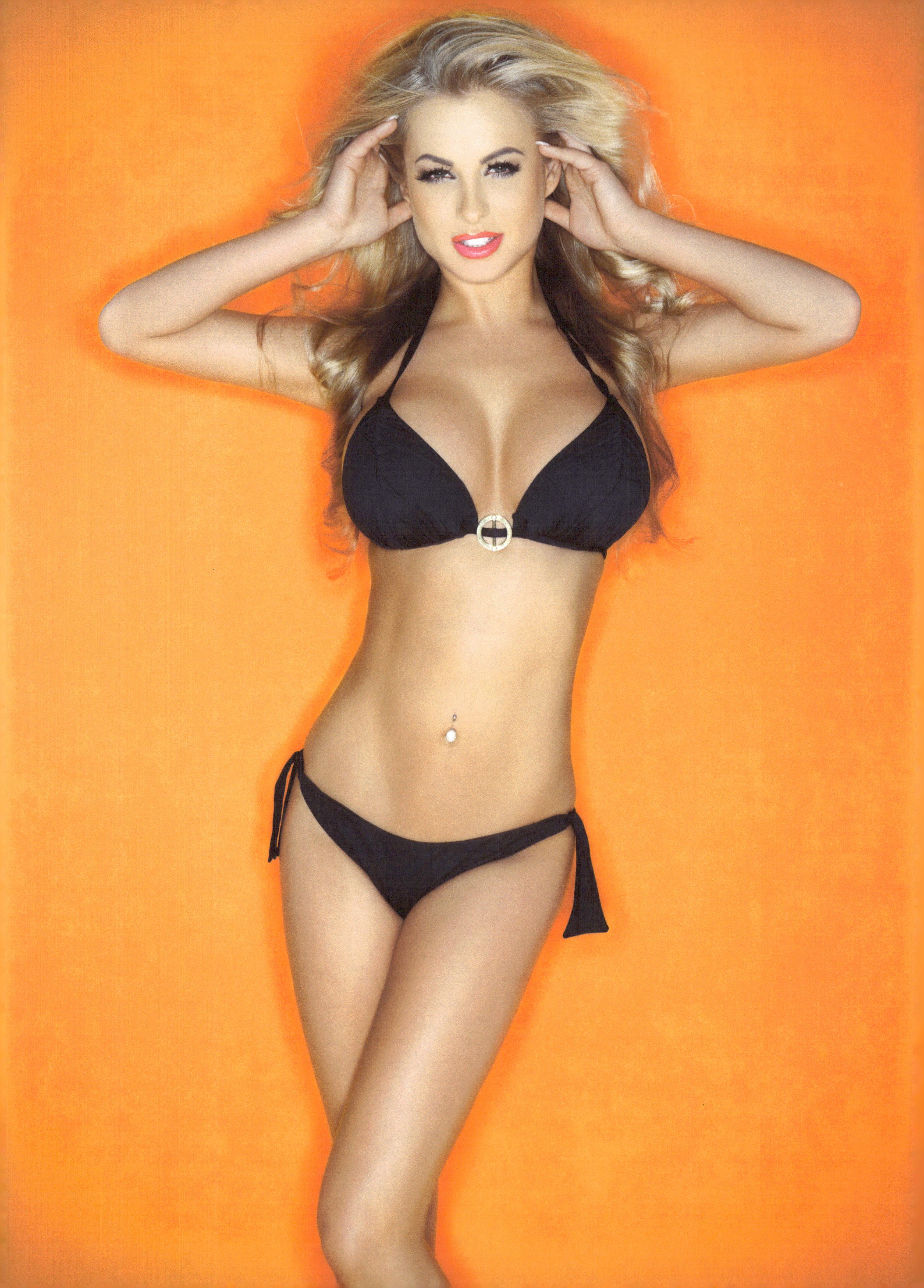

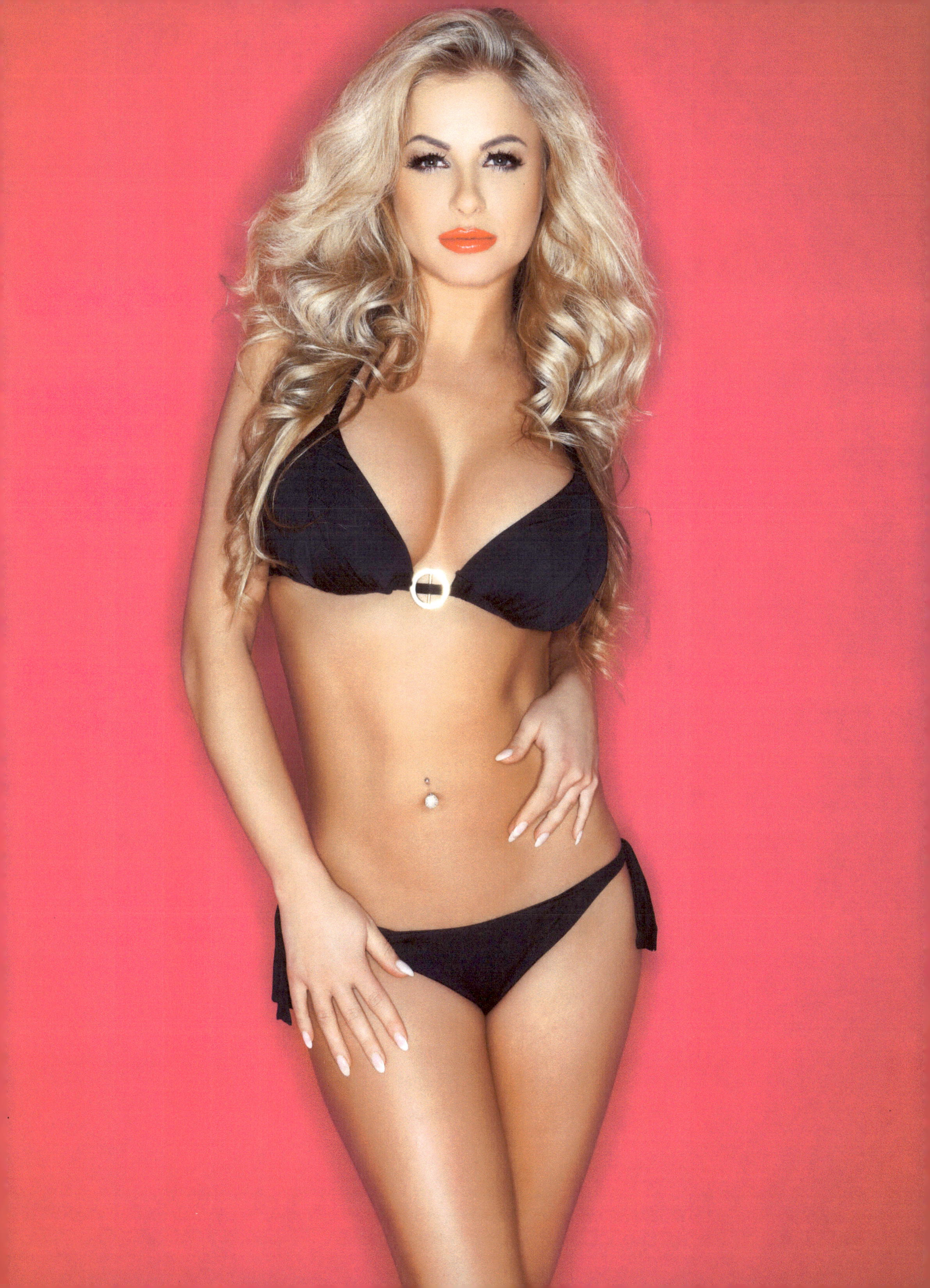

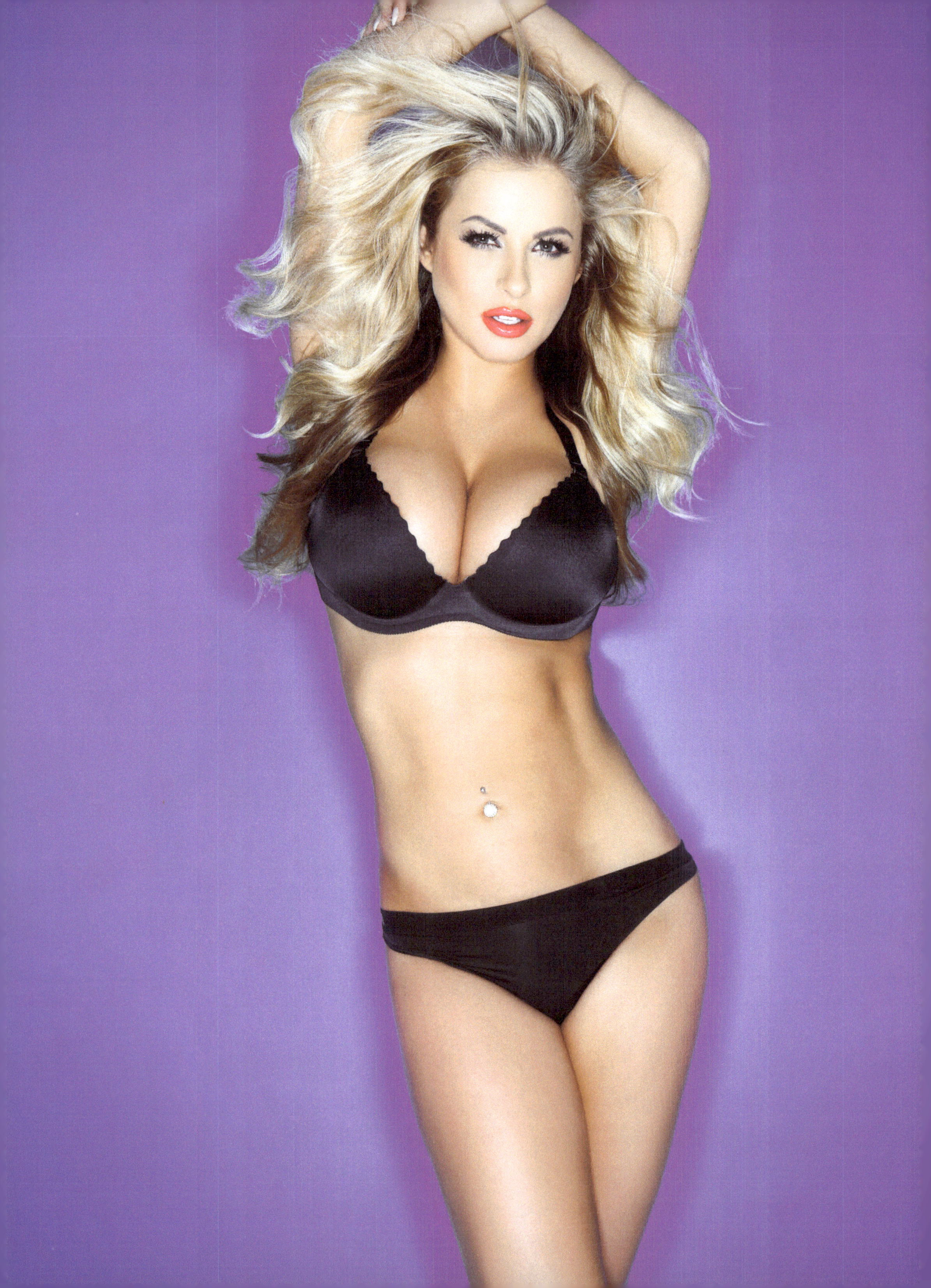

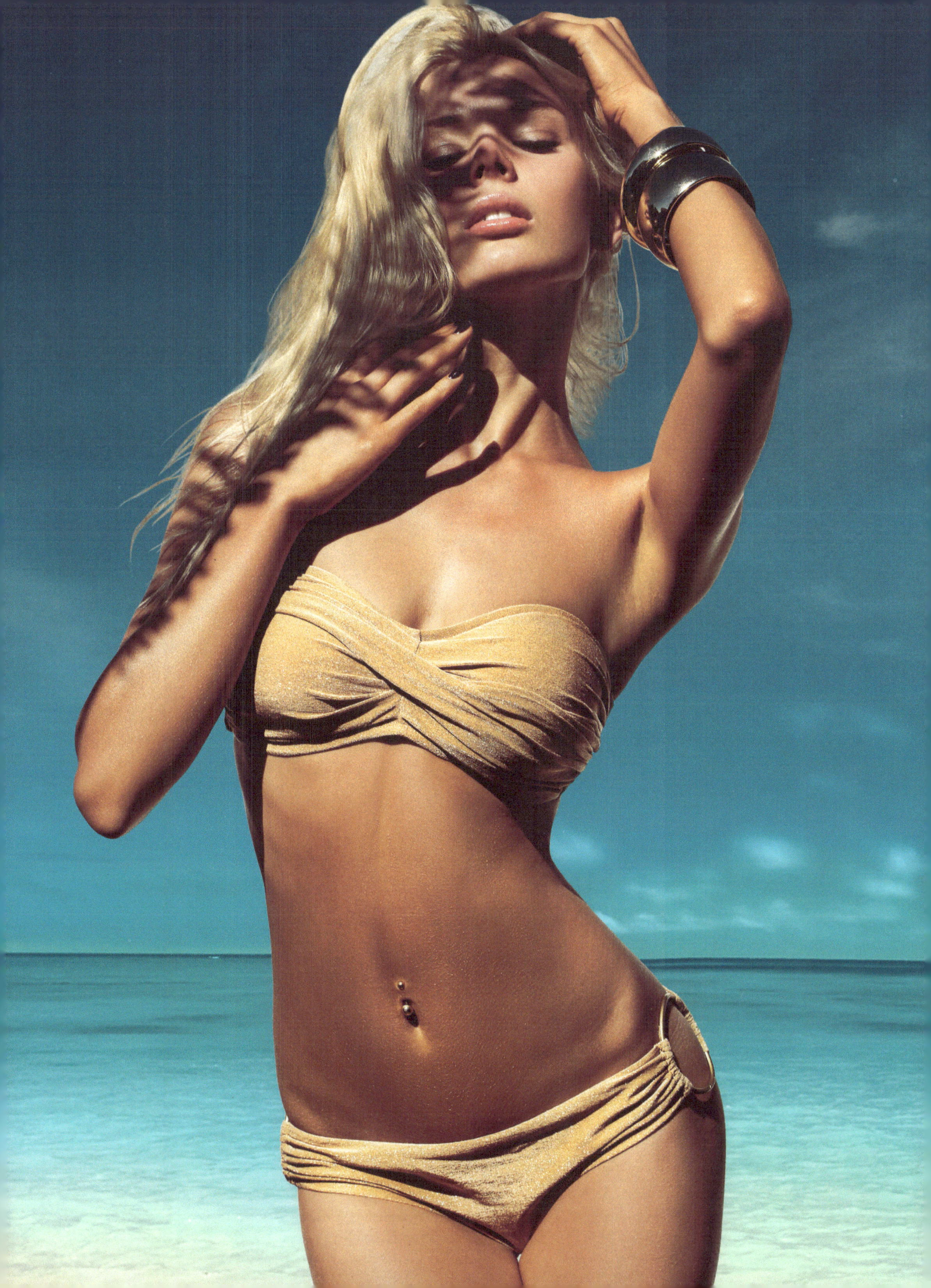

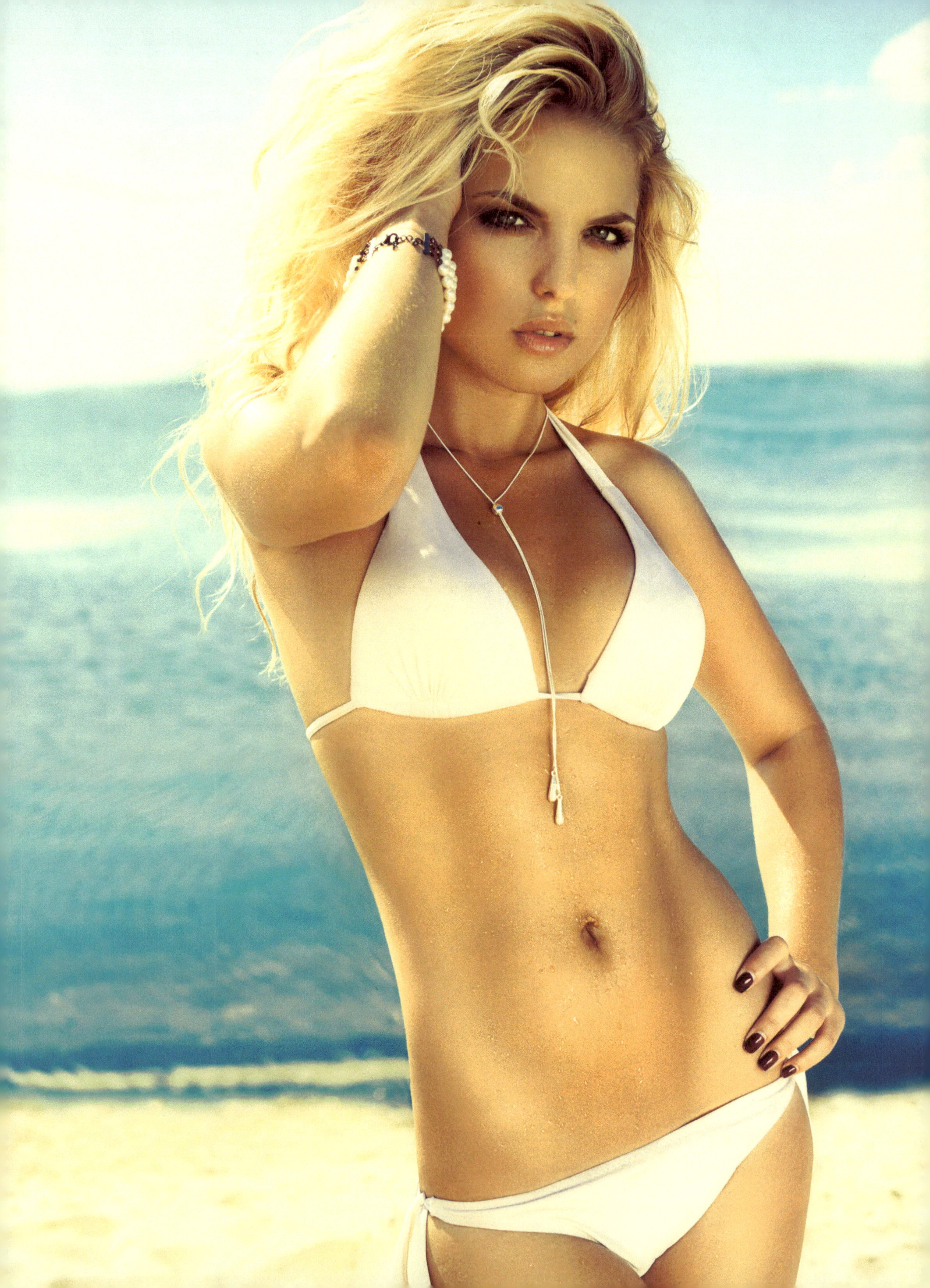

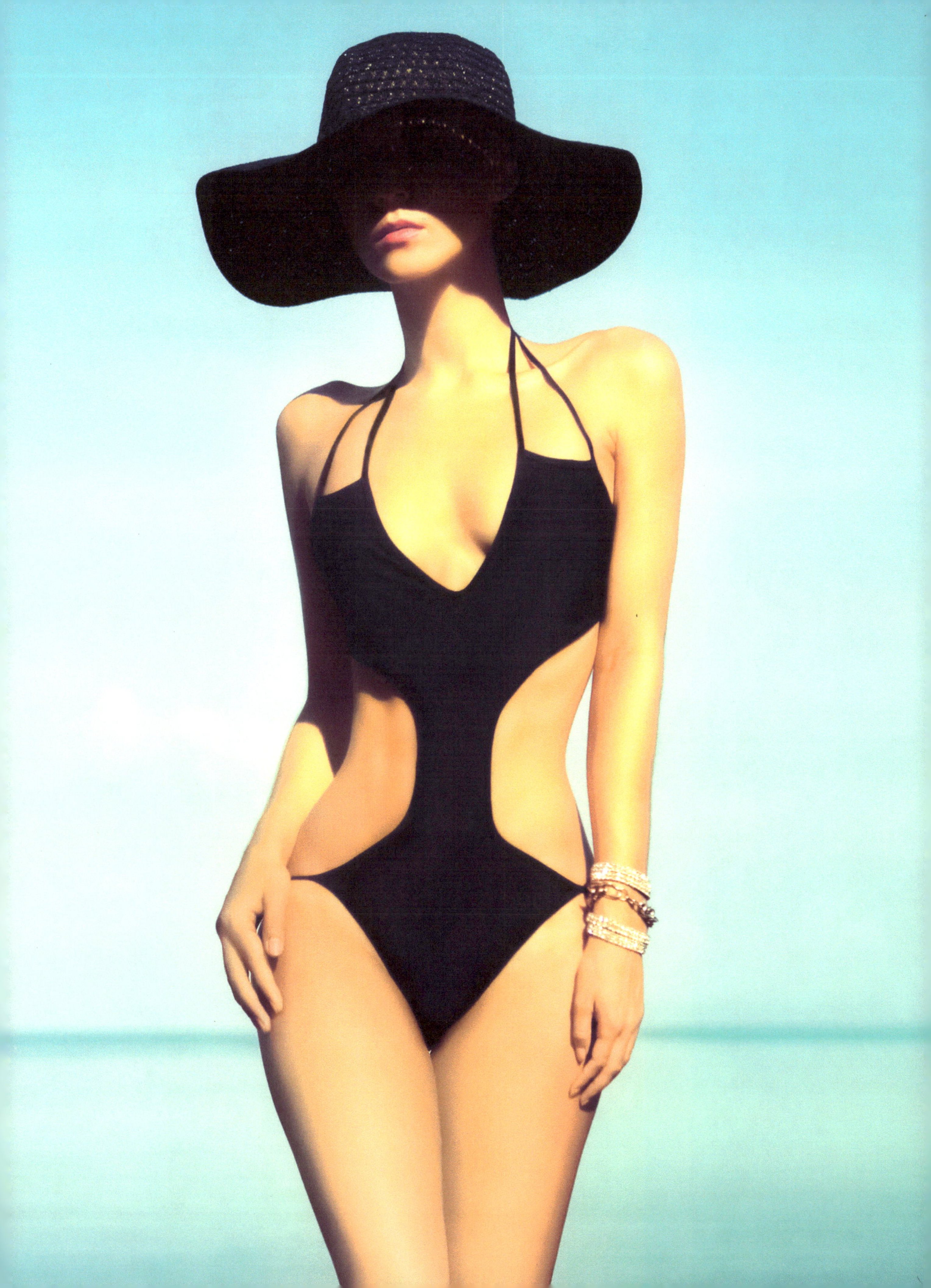

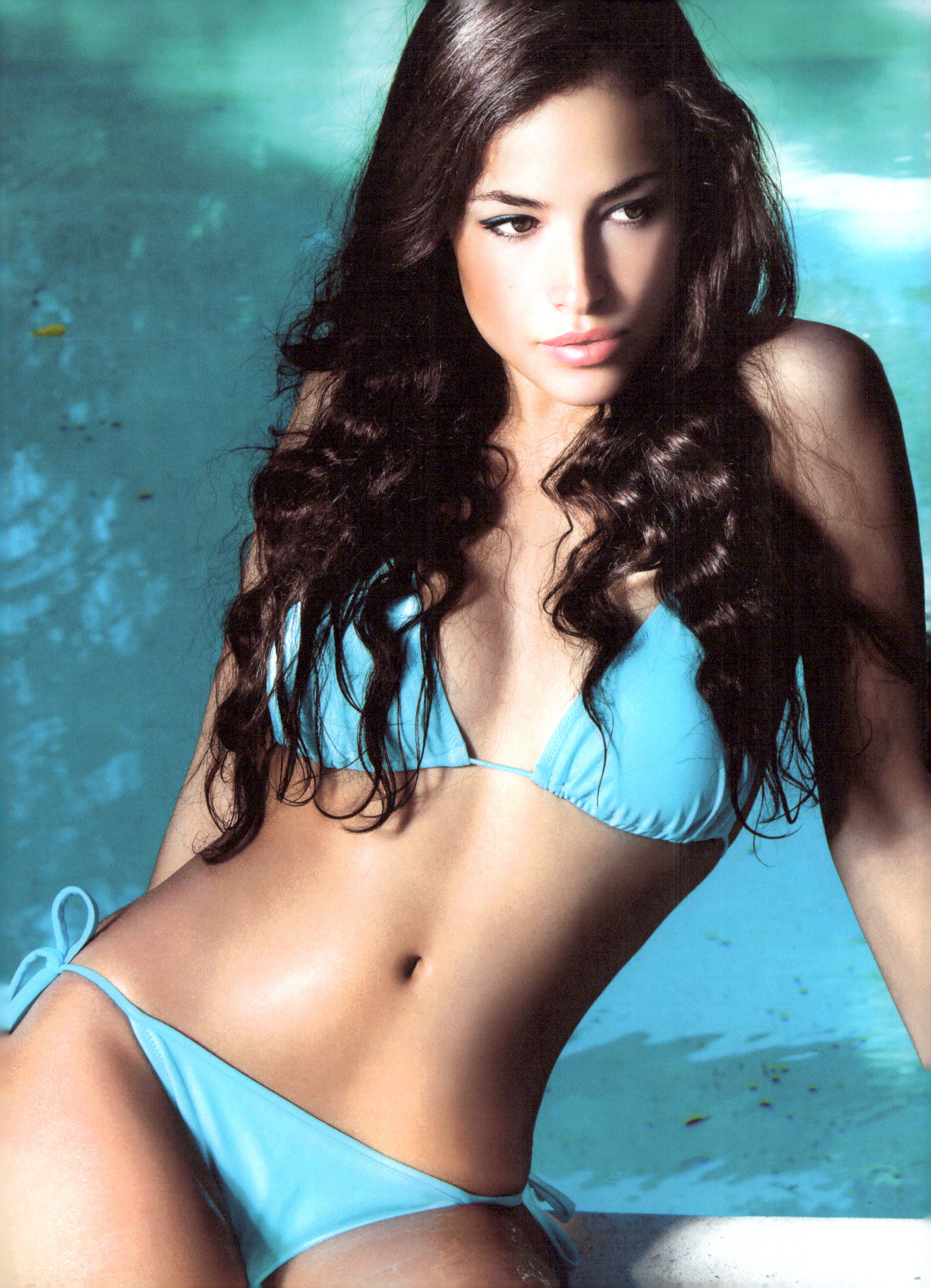

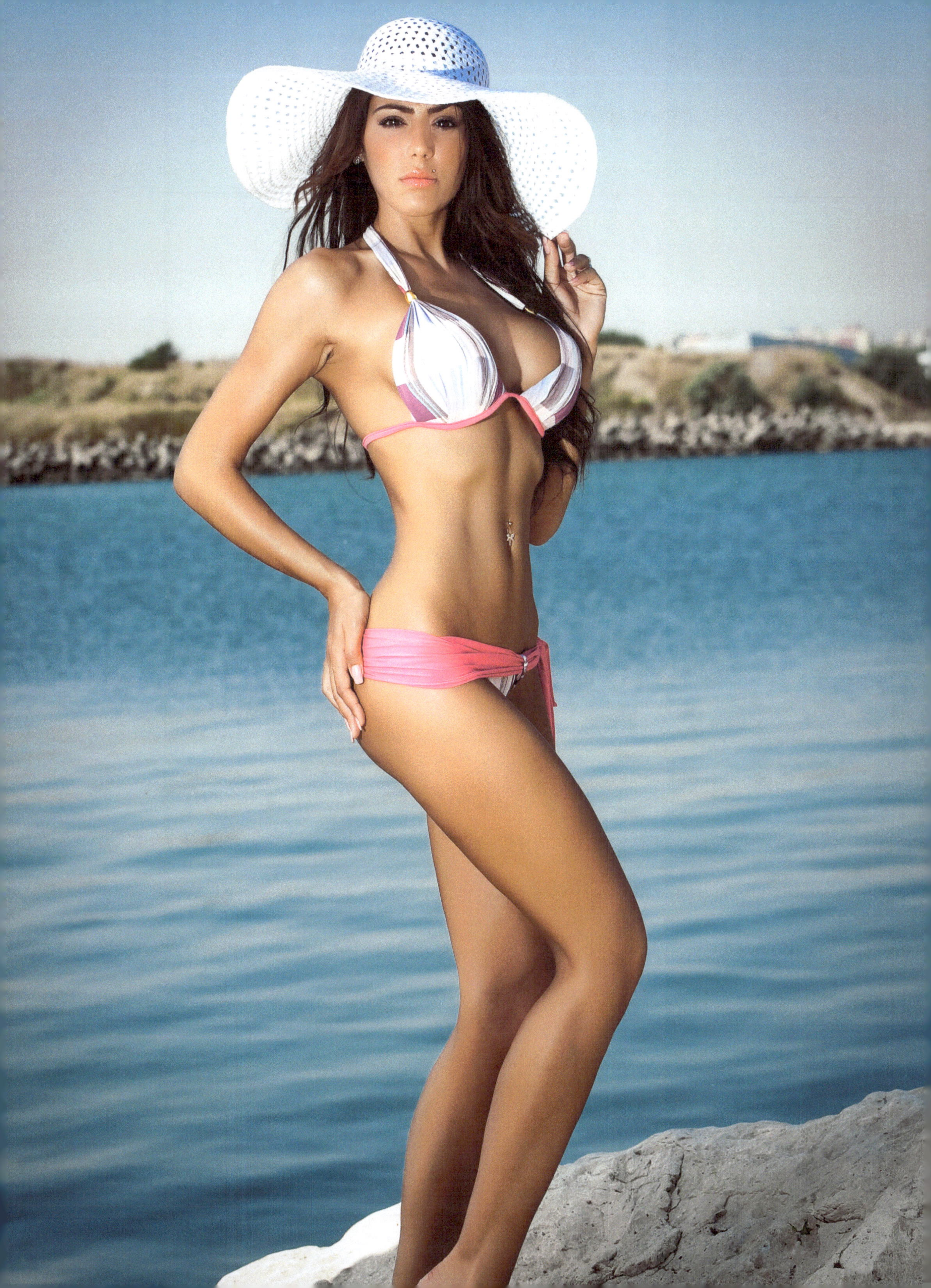

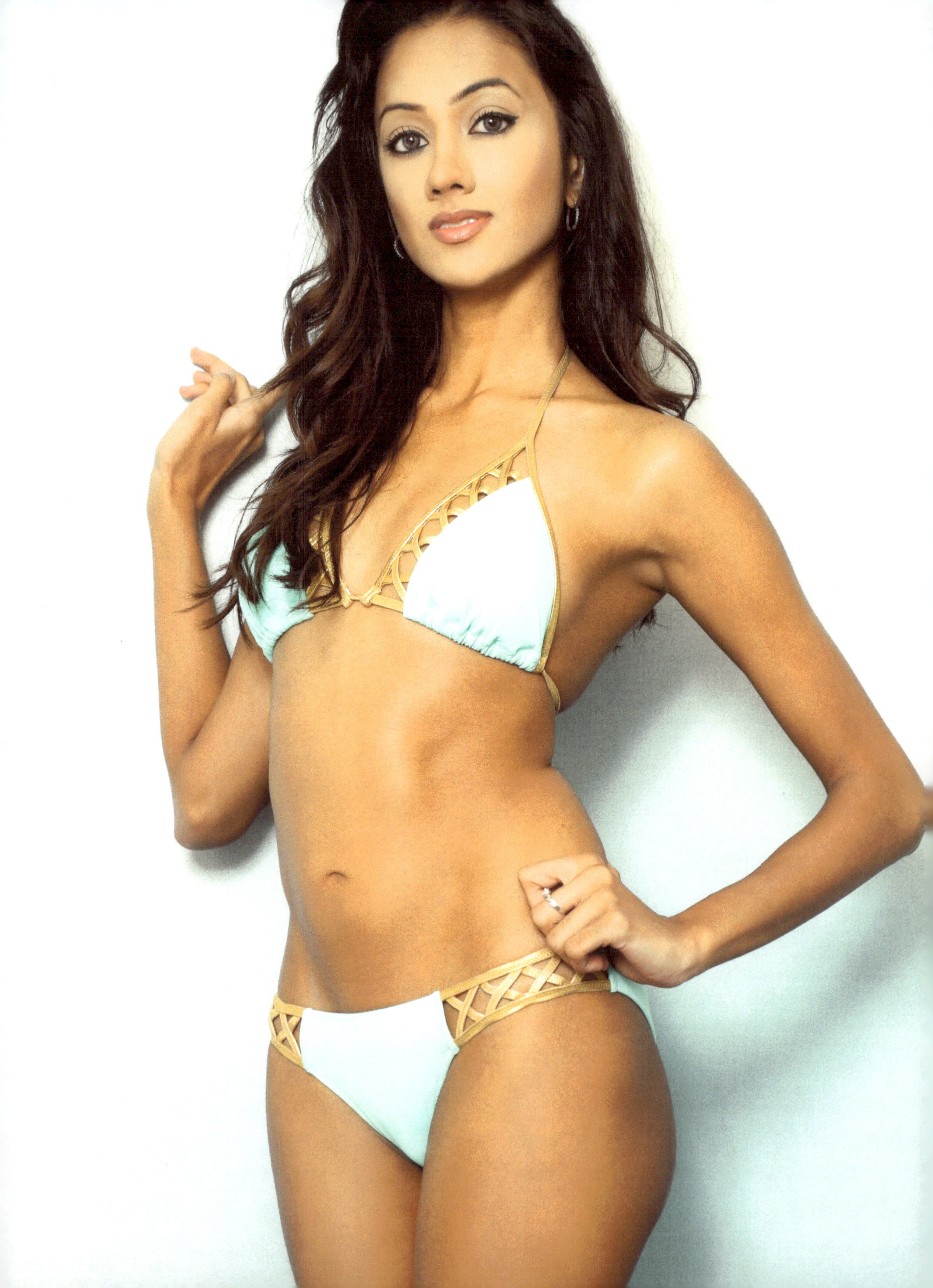

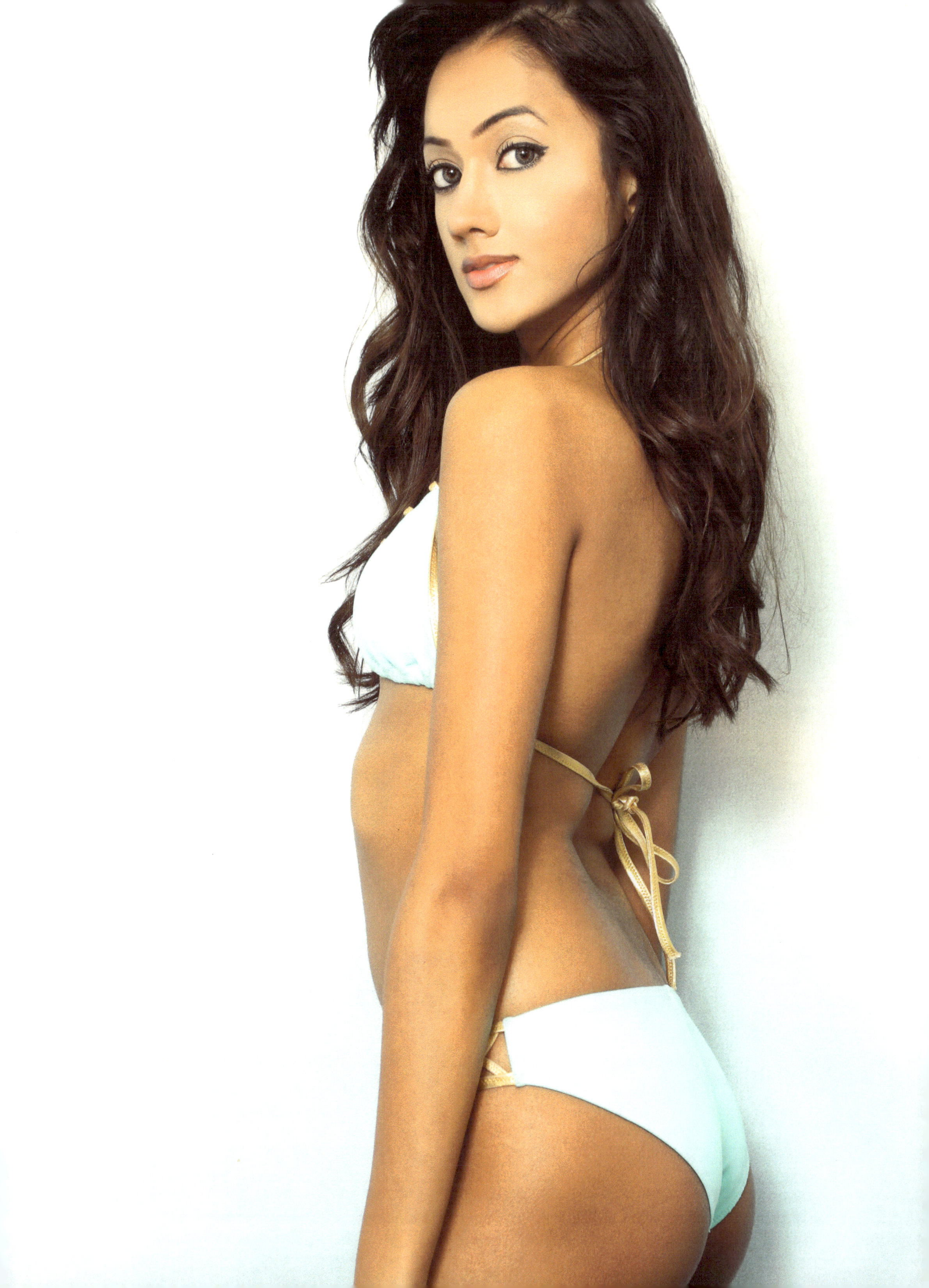

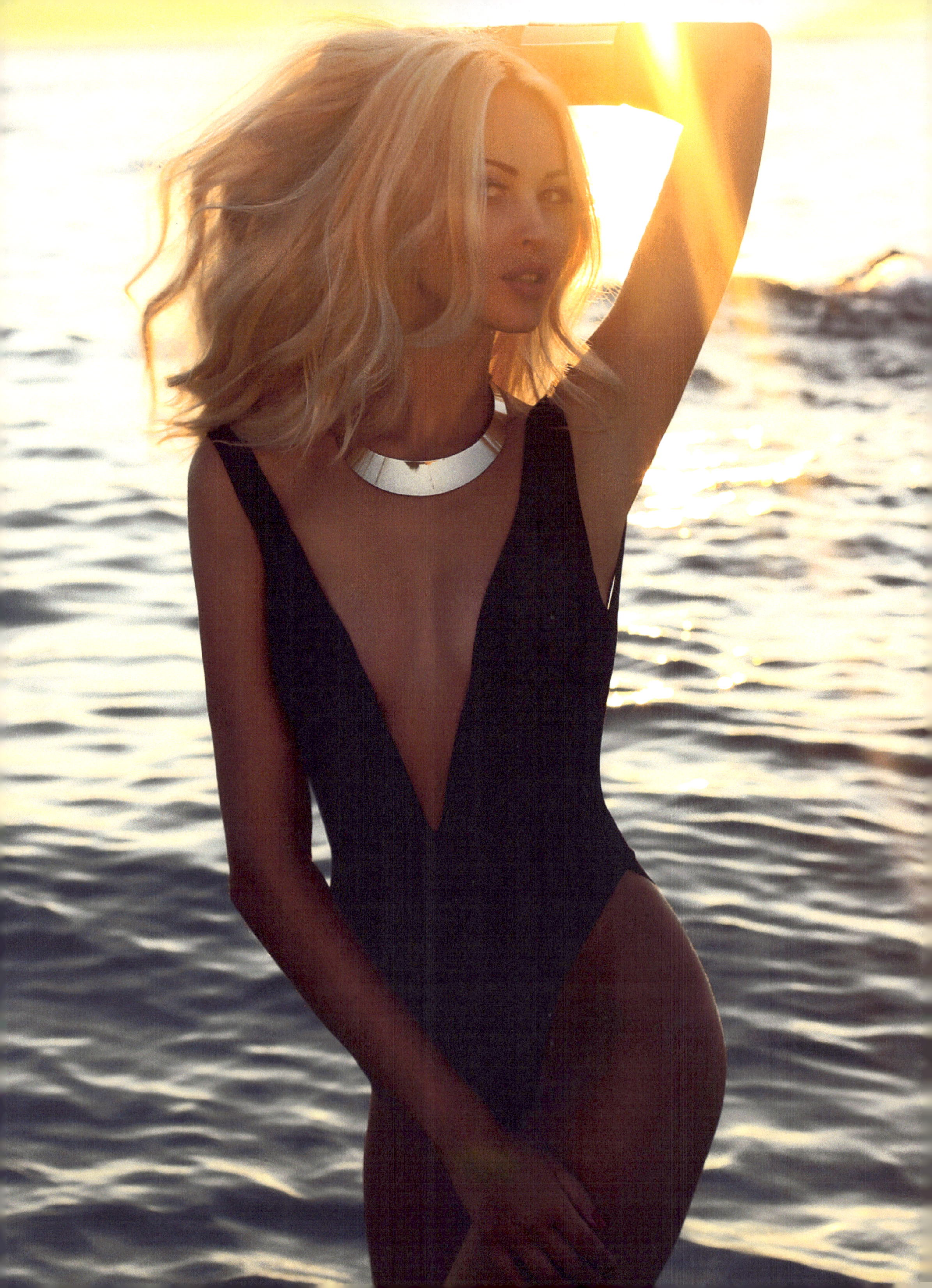

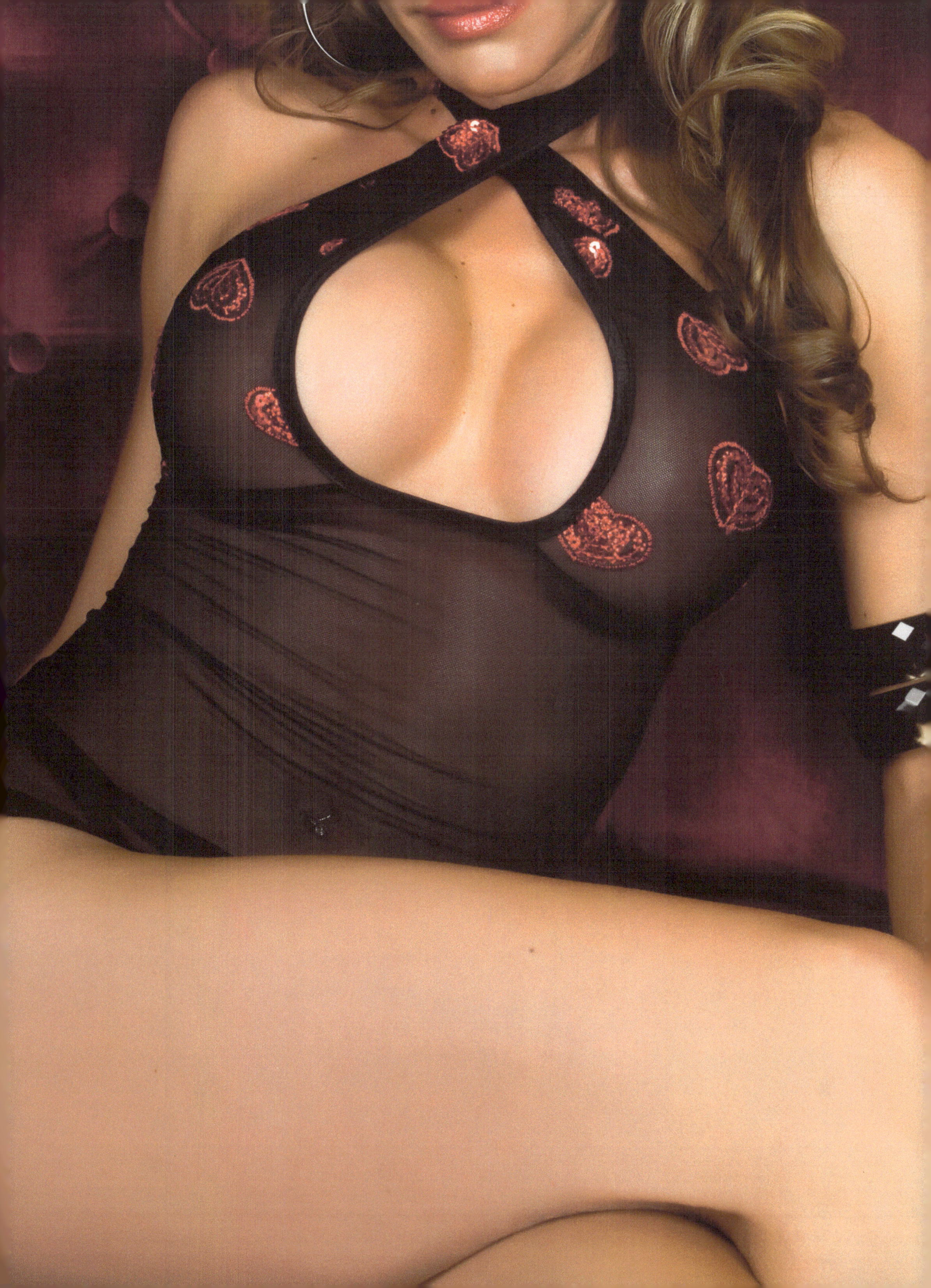

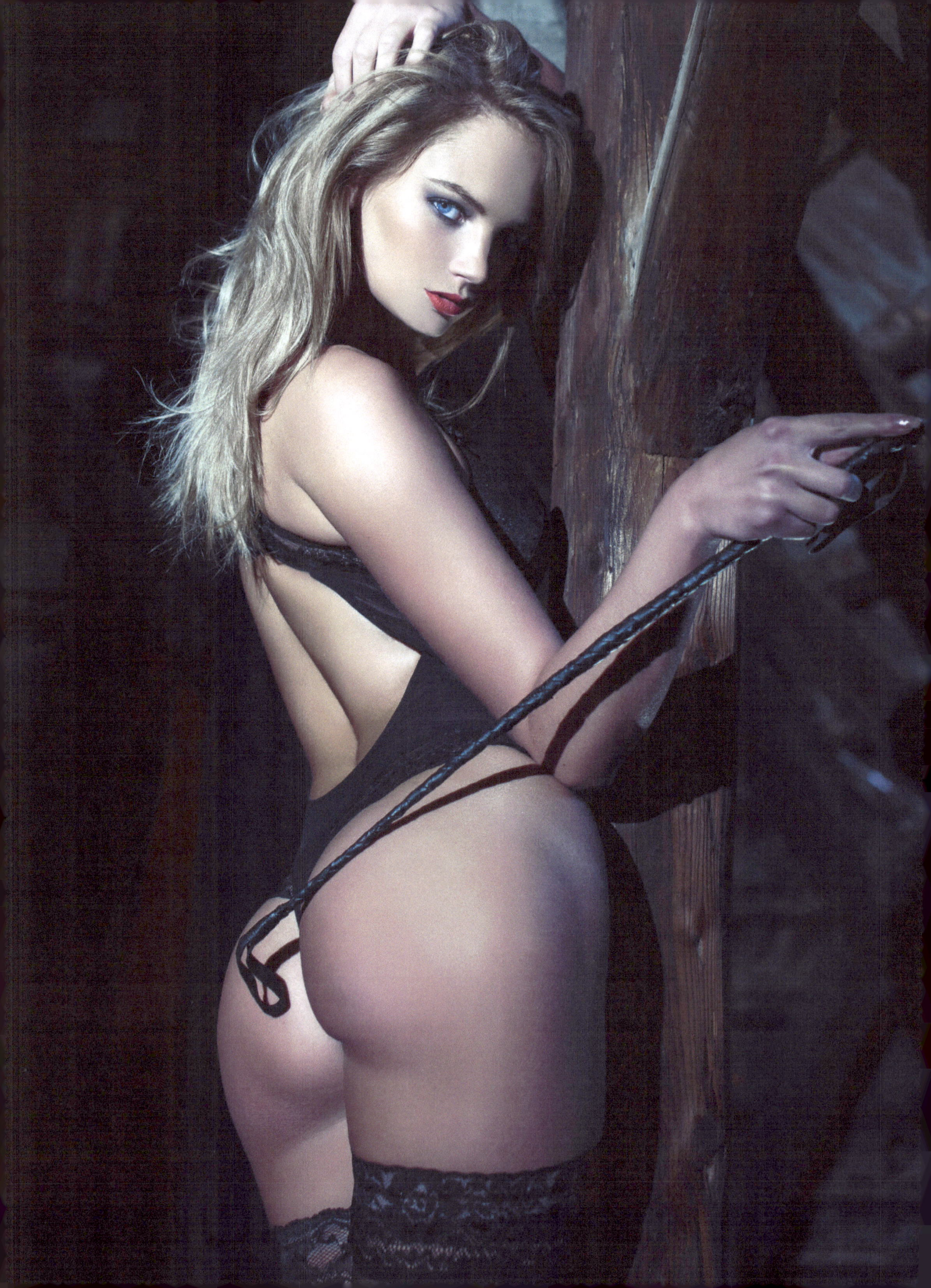

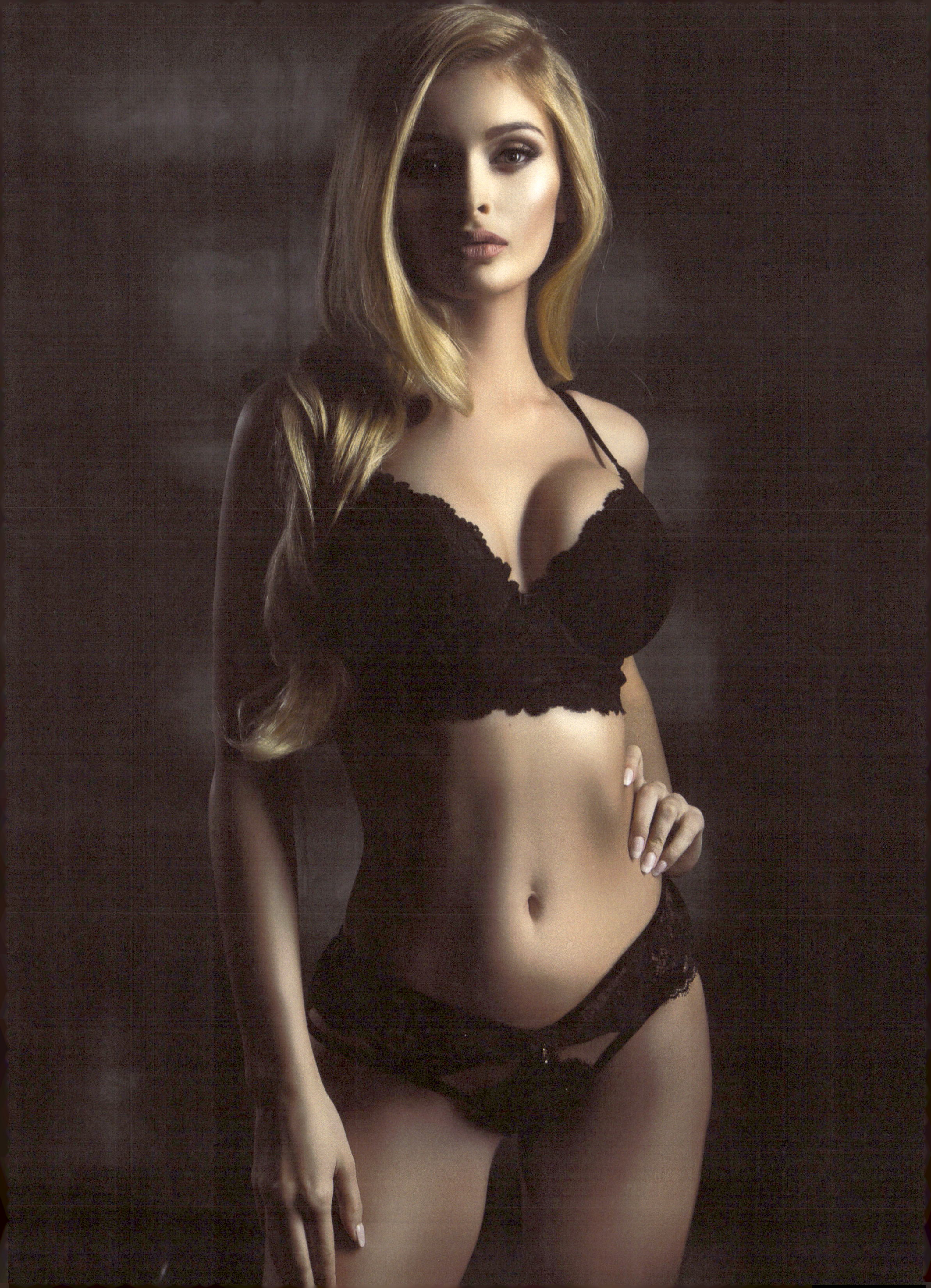

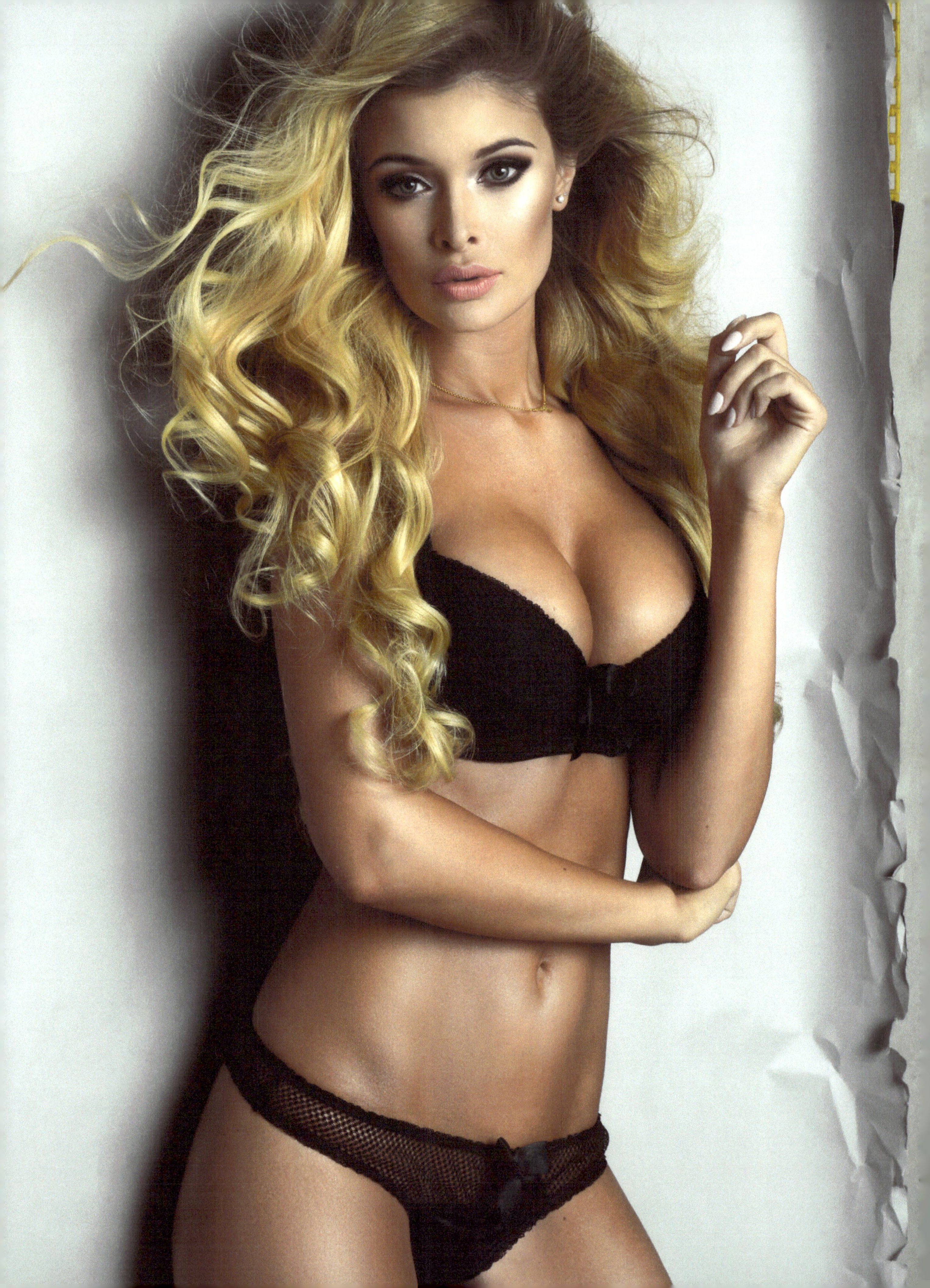

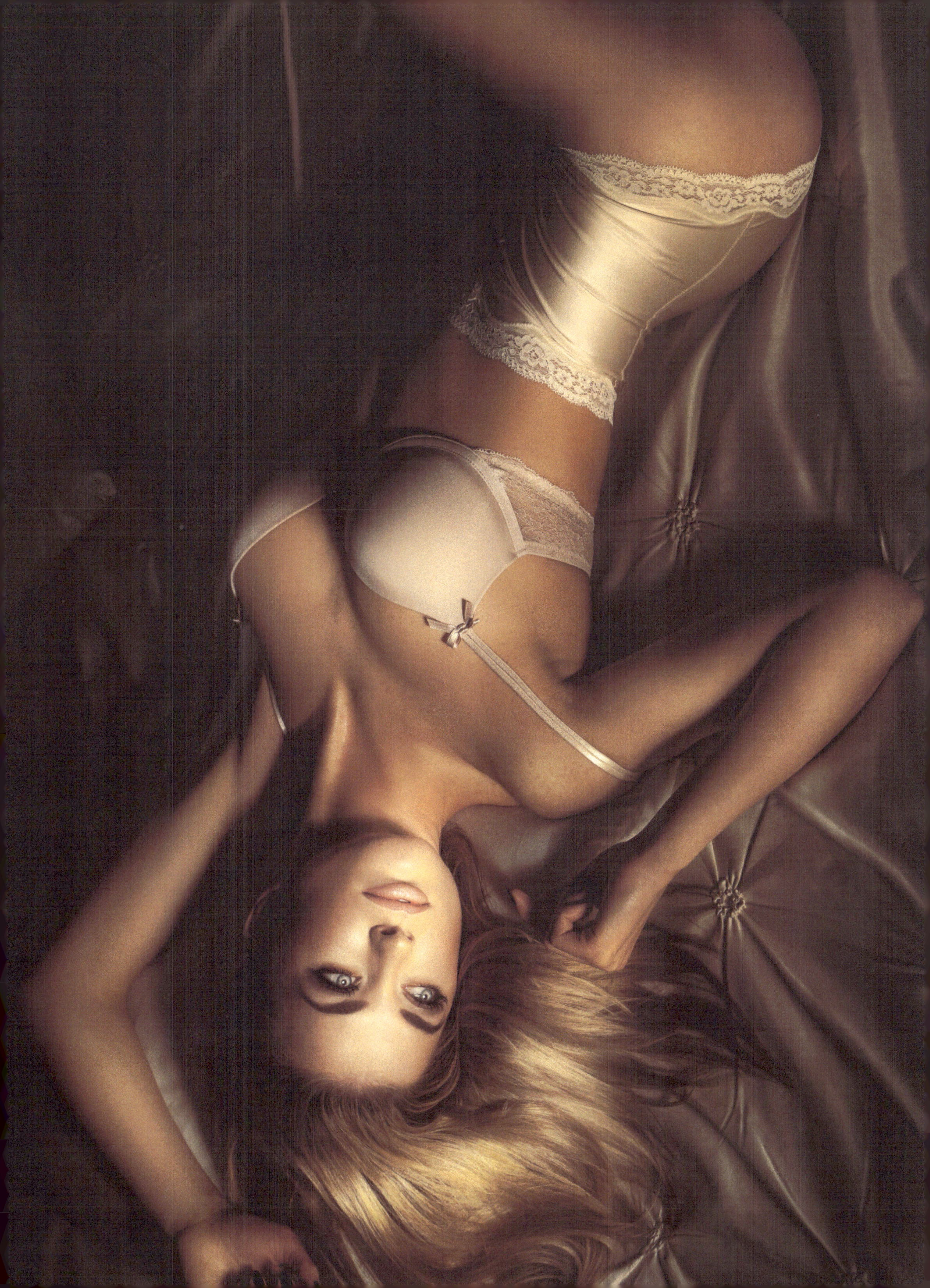

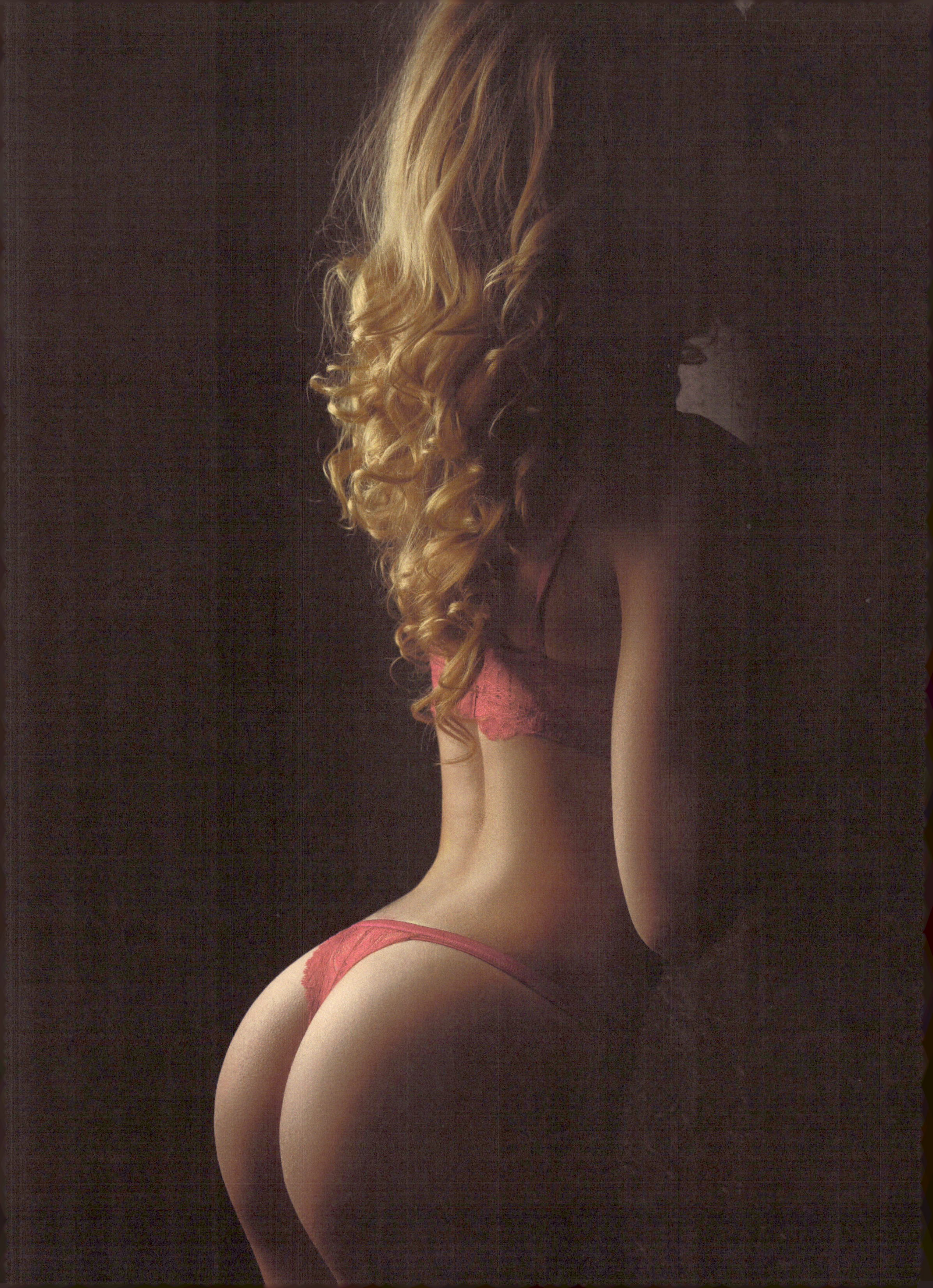

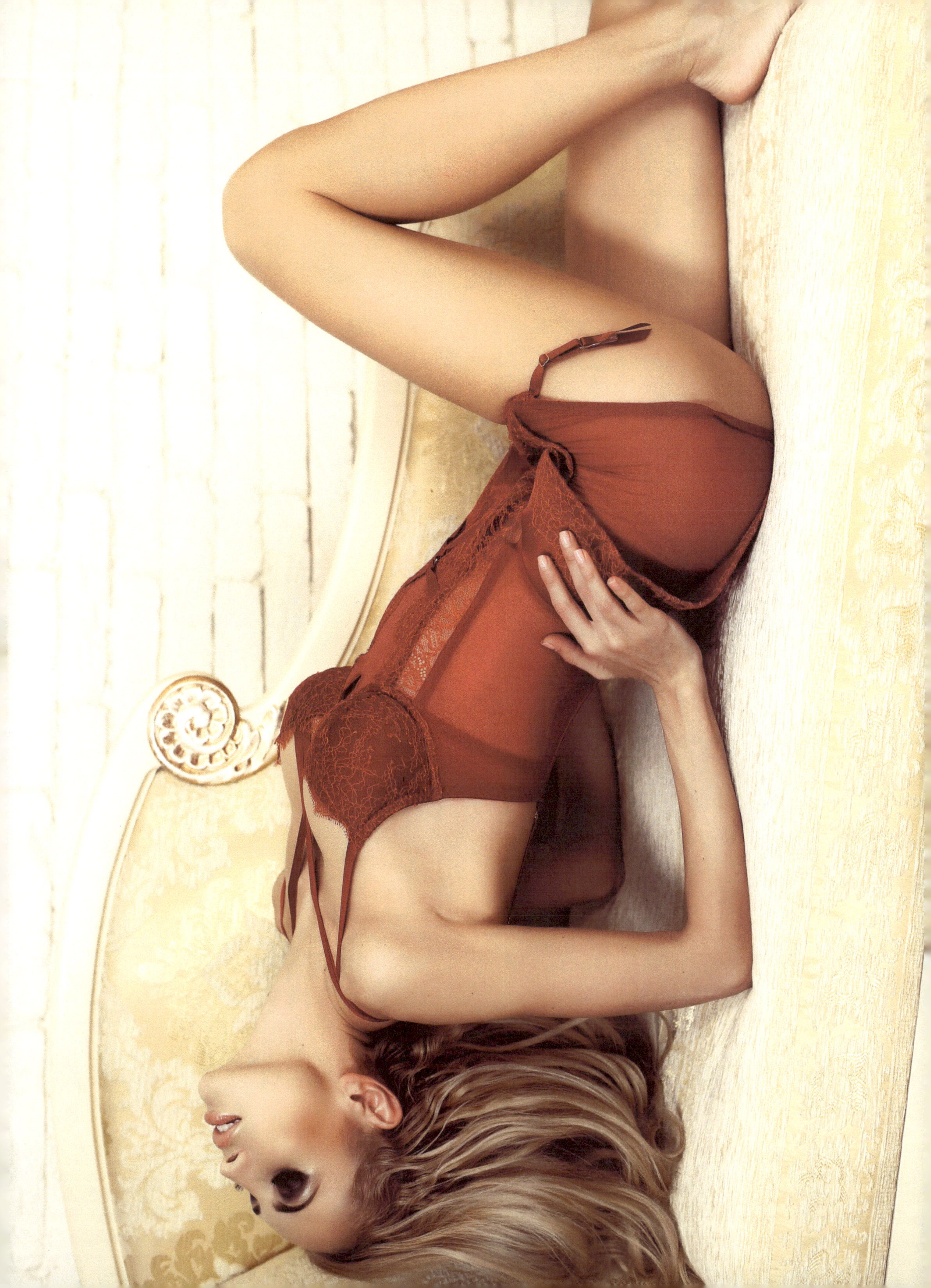

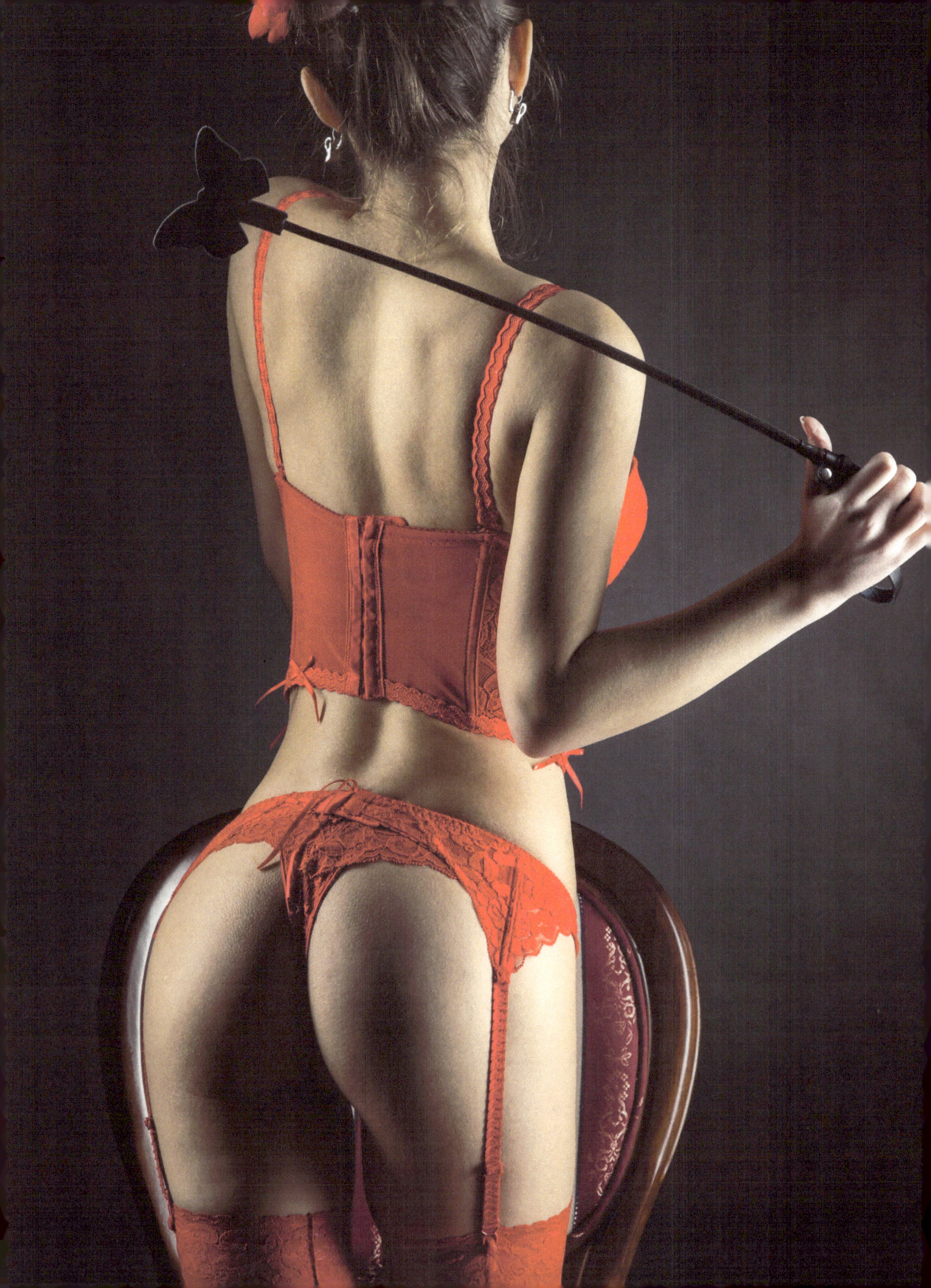

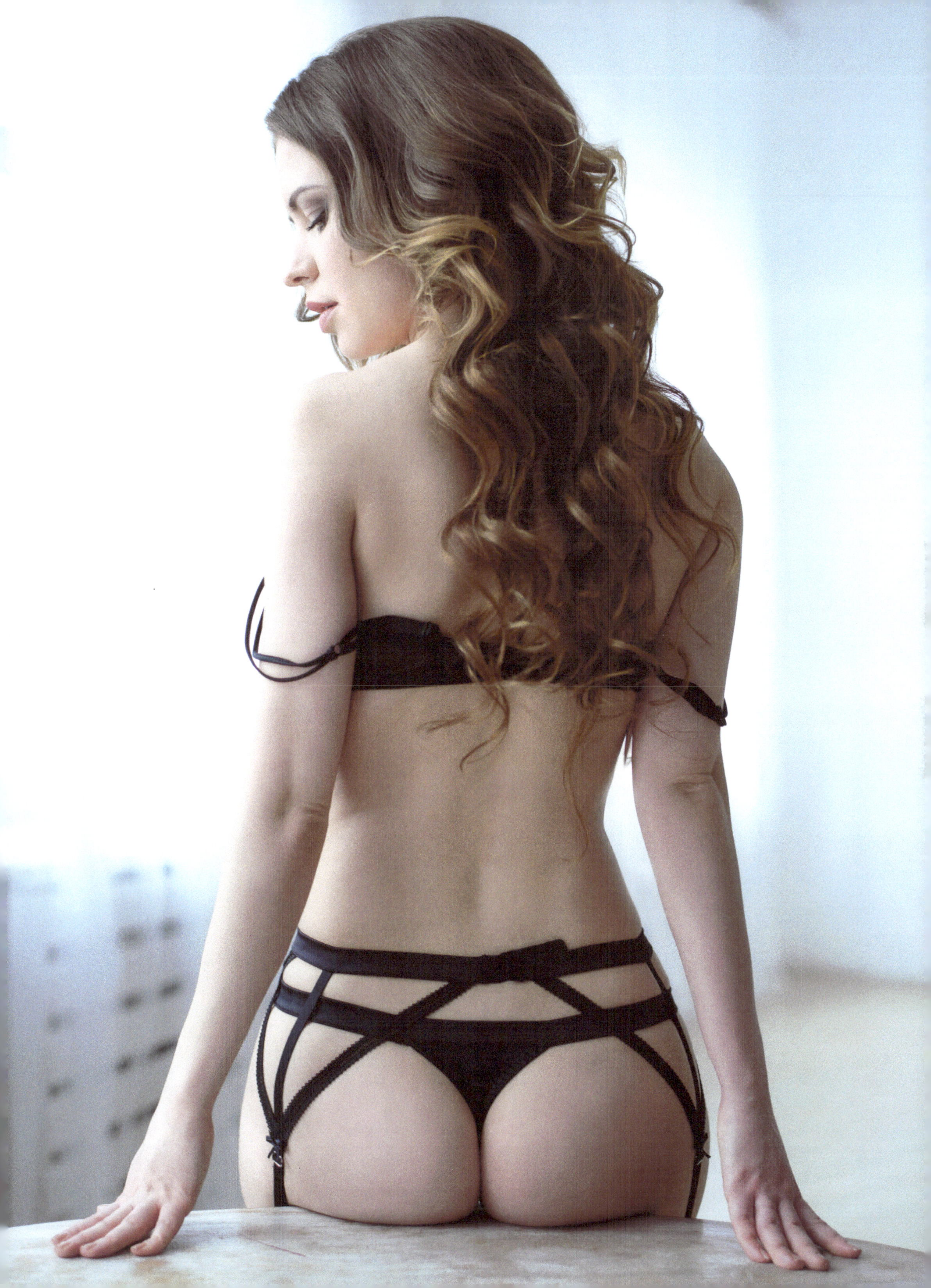

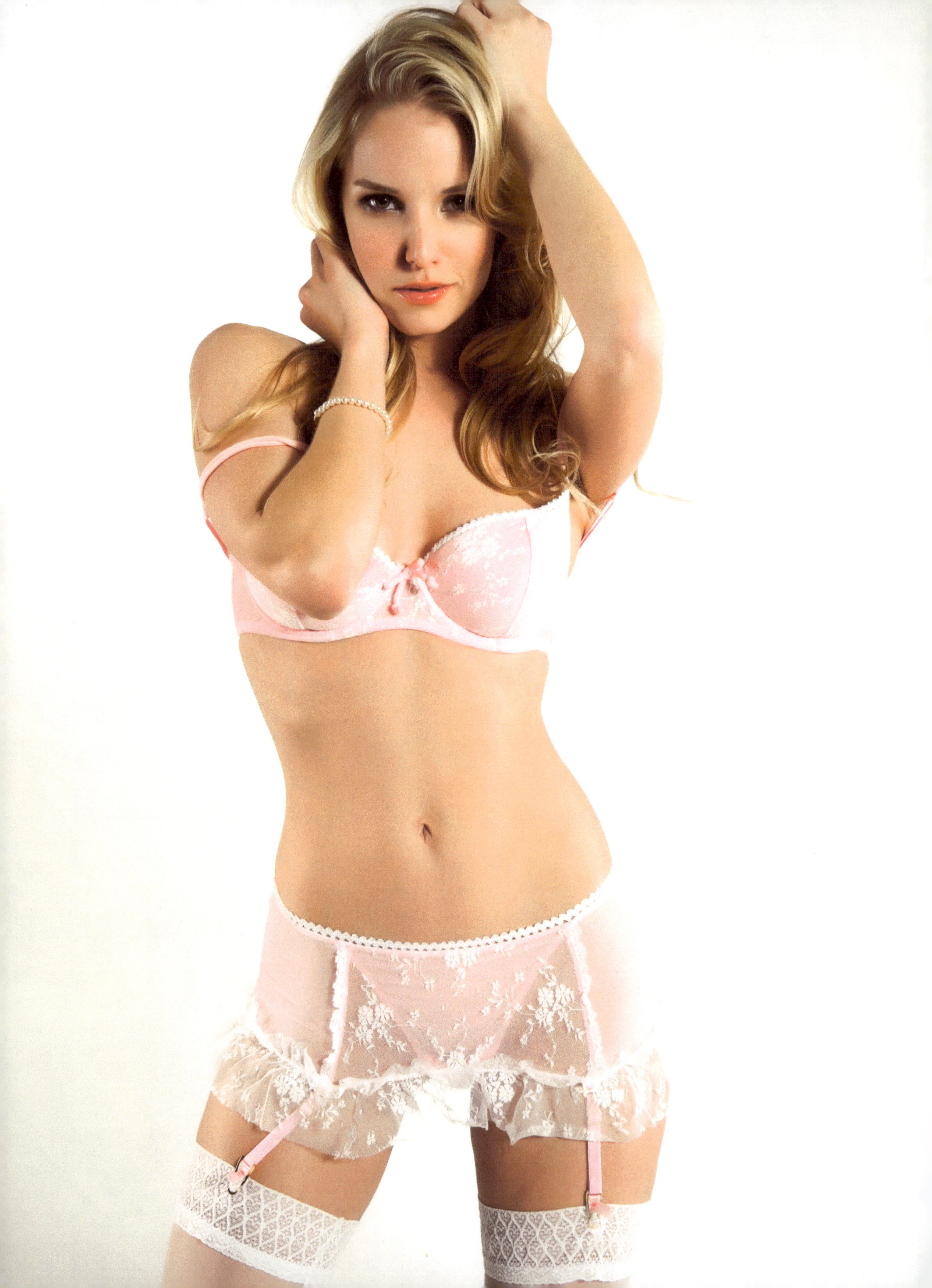

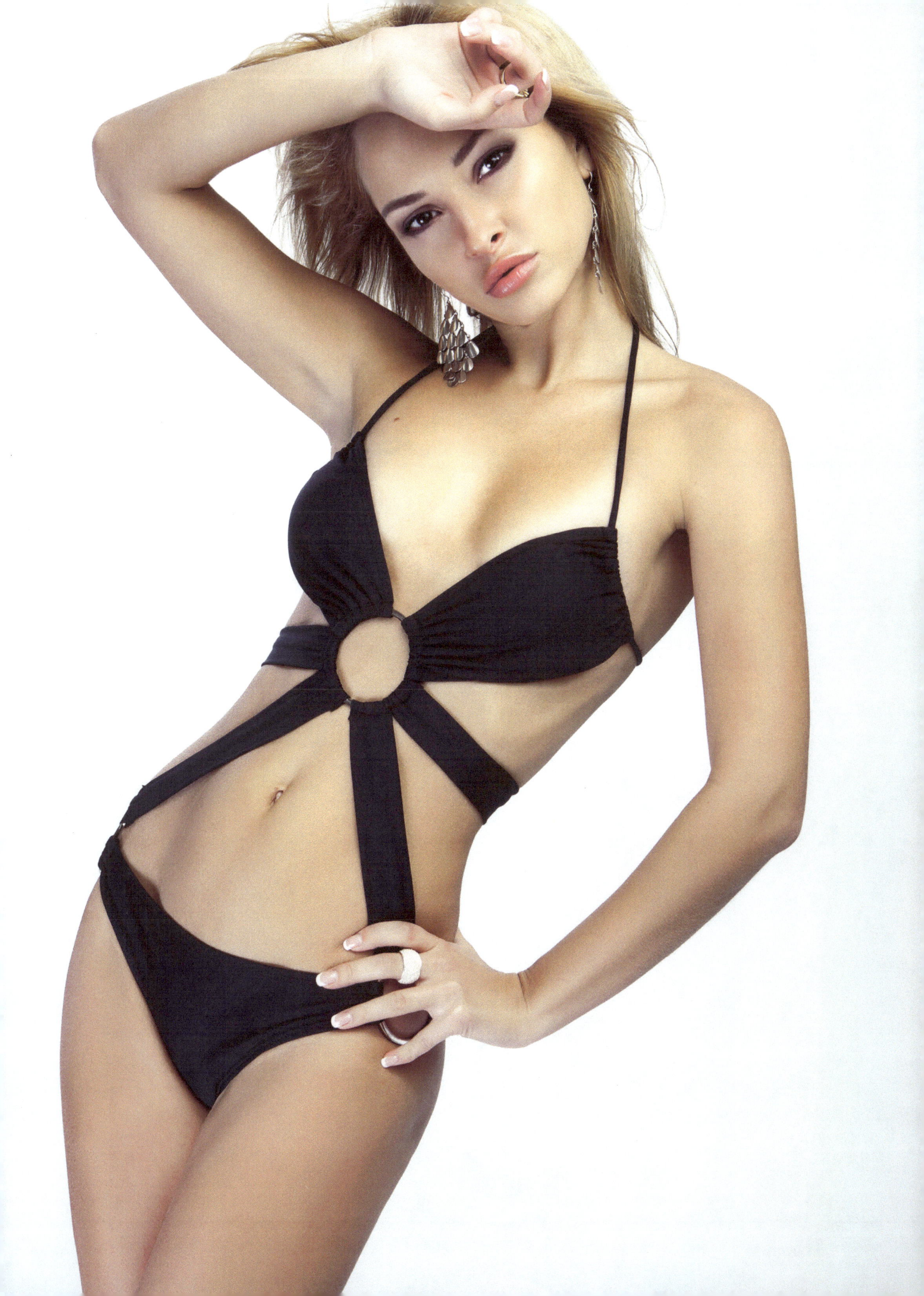

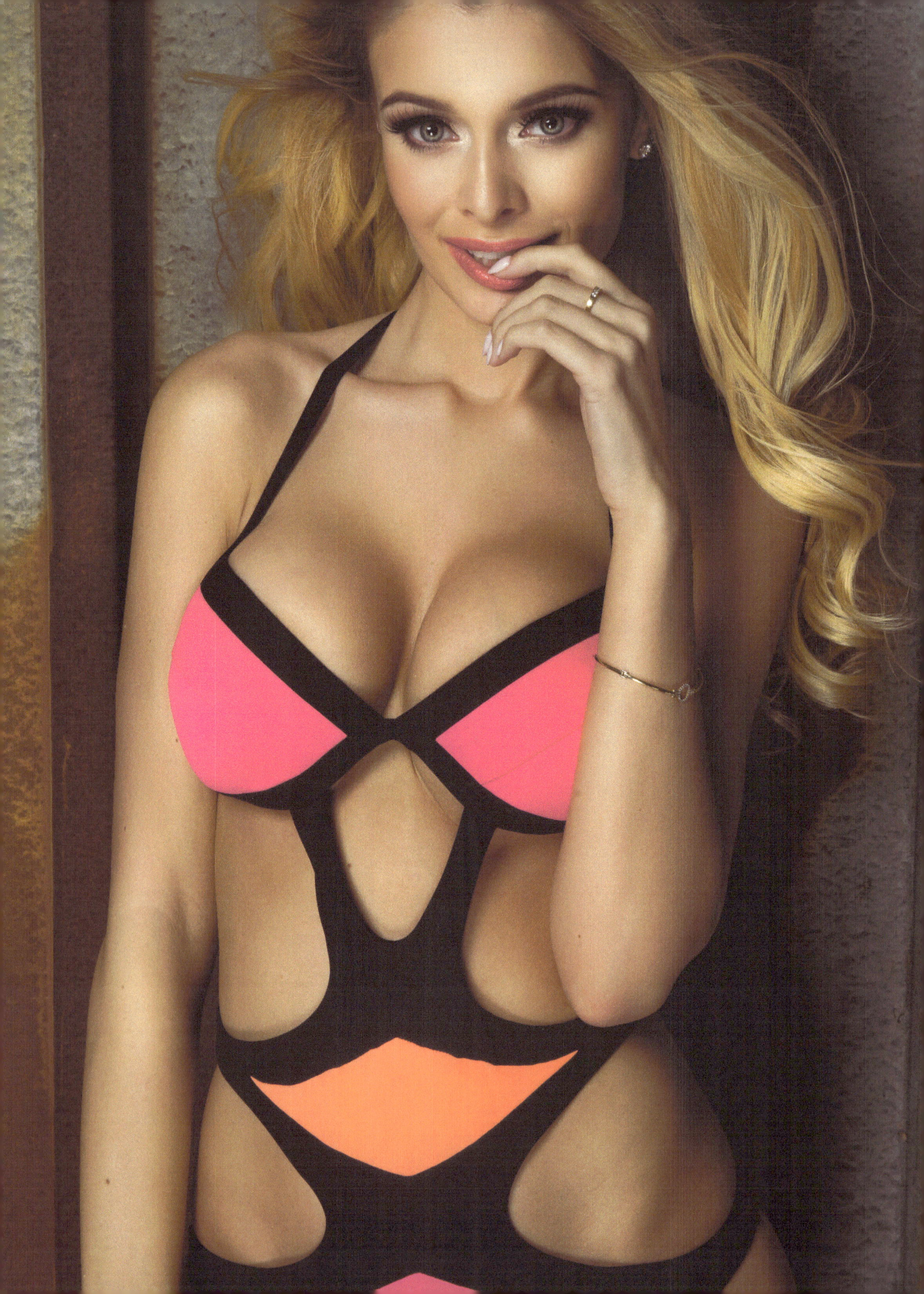

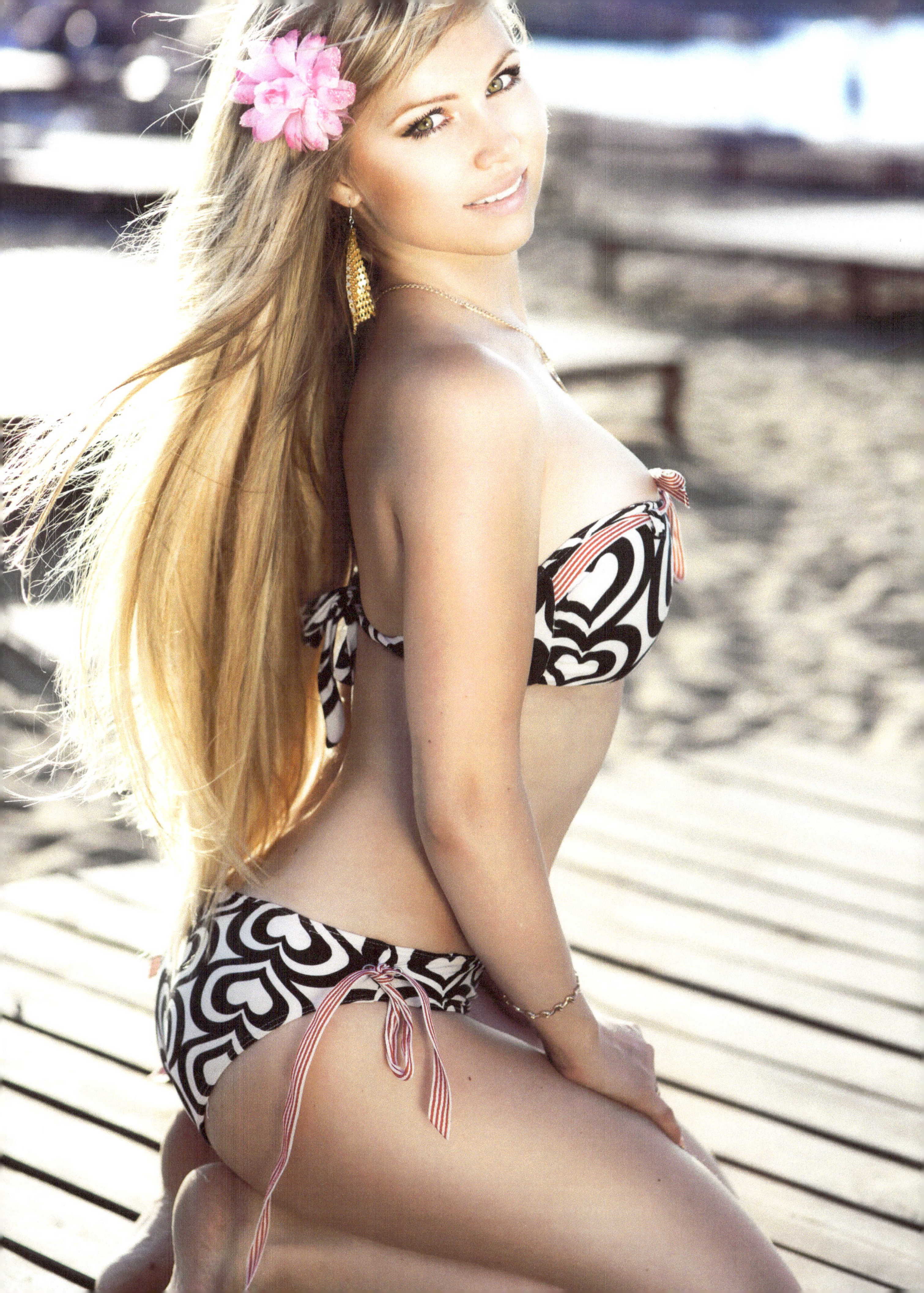

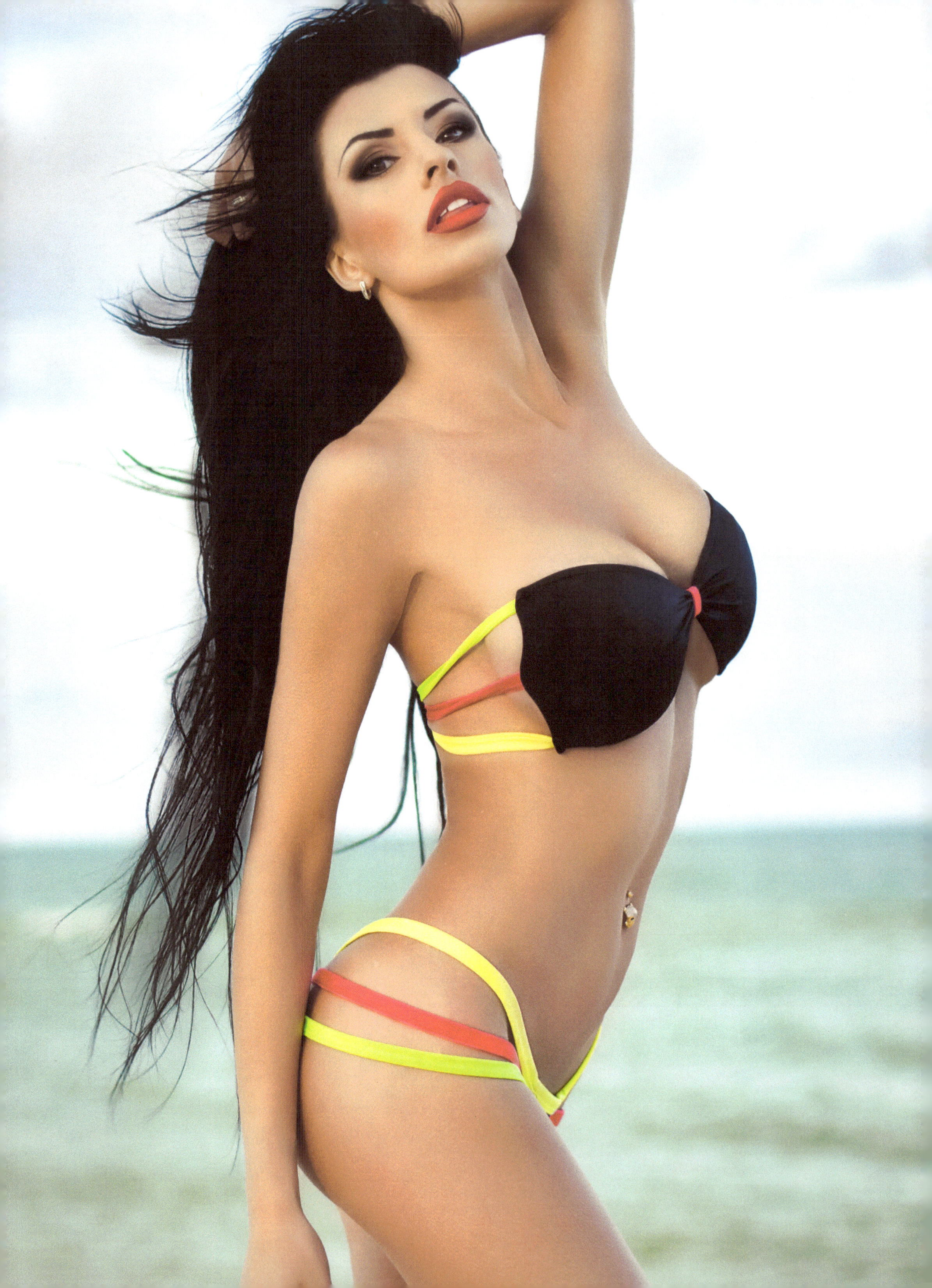

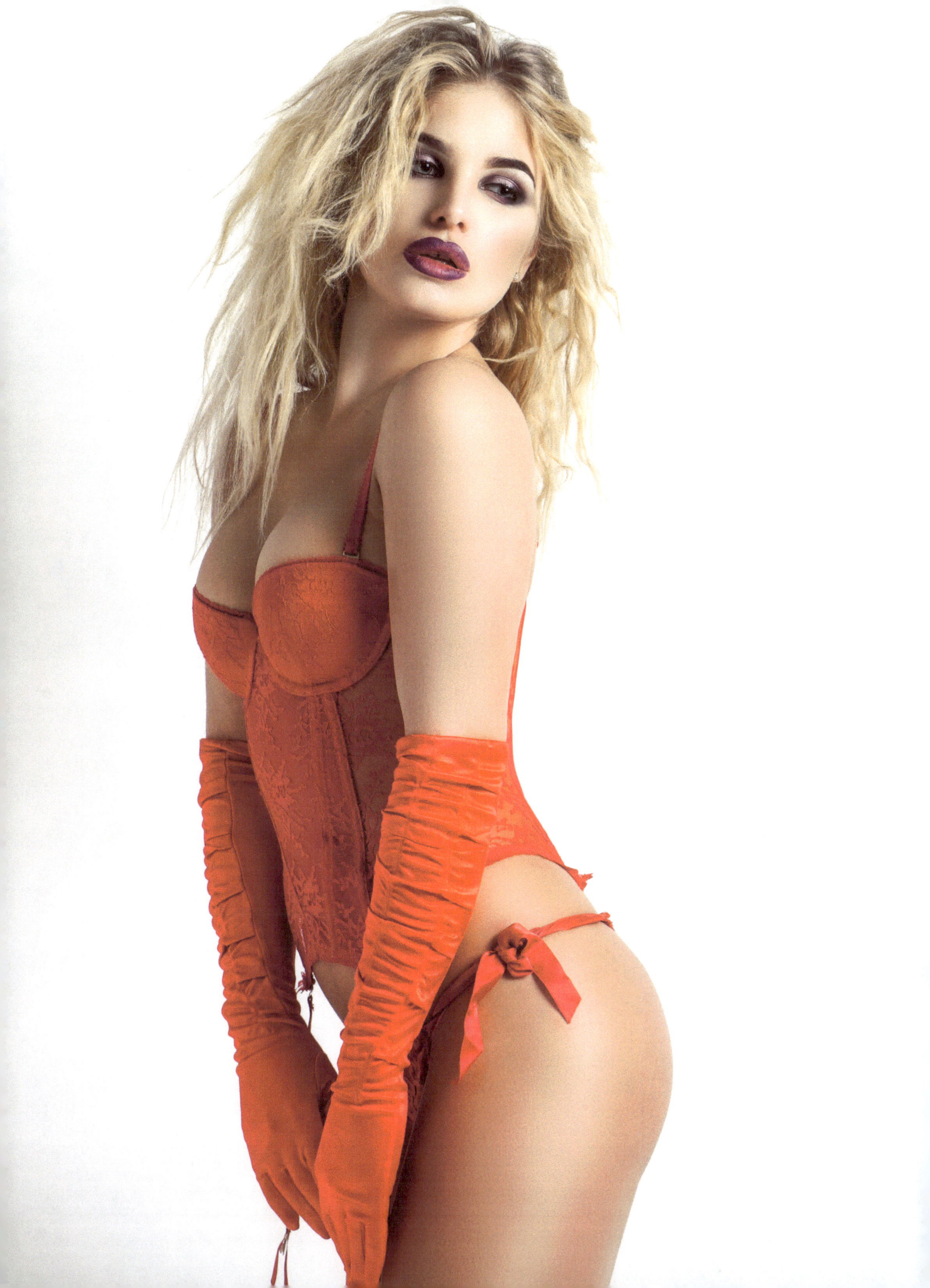

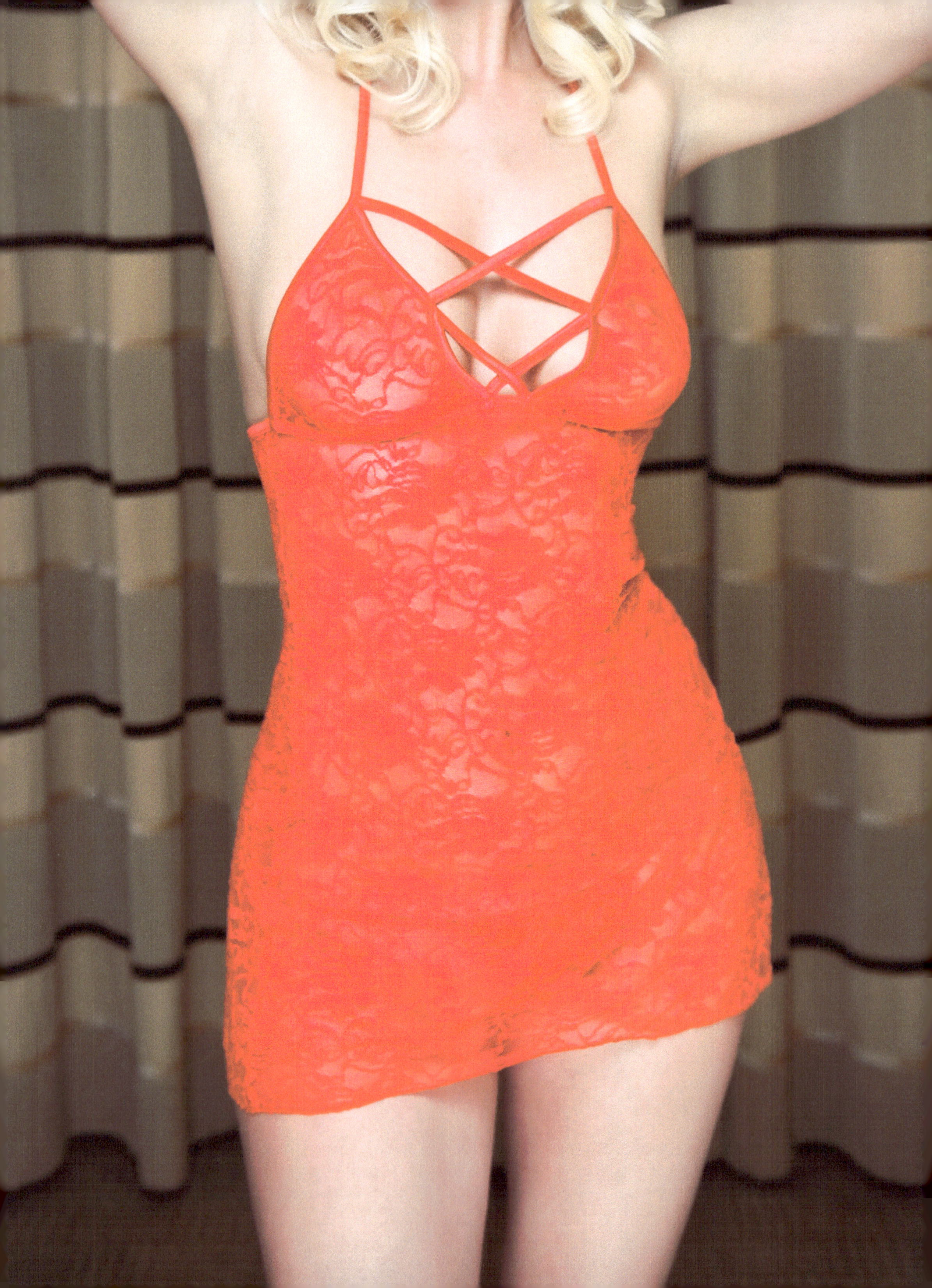

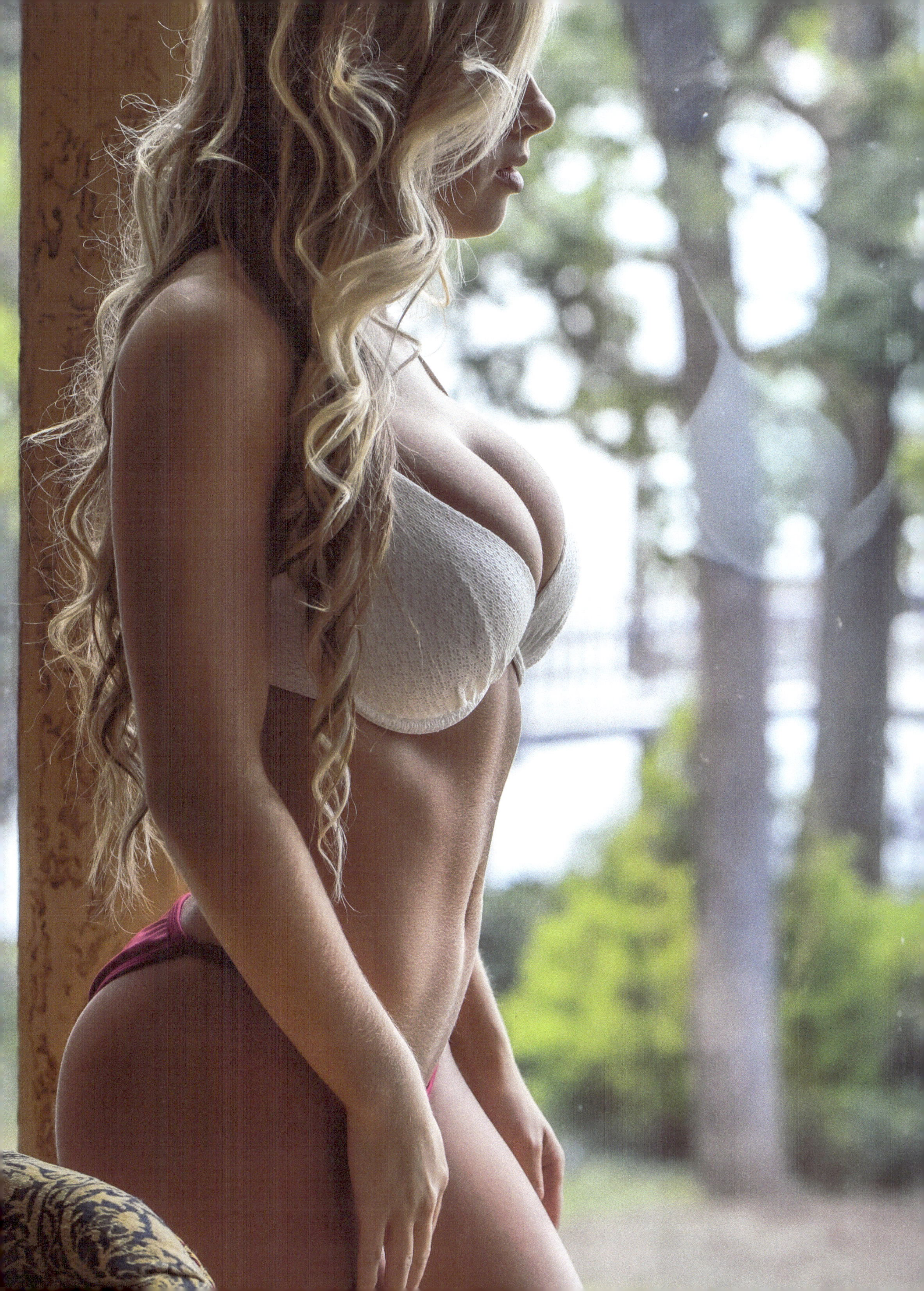

www.ingramcontent.com/pod-product-compliance
Lightning Source LLC
Chambersburg PA
CBHW050421180526
45159CB00005B/2361
9781539626305